...IF YOU LIVED
in Colonial Times

by Ann McGovern

illustrated by June Otani

SCHOLASTIC INC.
New York   Toronto   London   Auckland   Sydney

For Peter McGovern

ISBN 0-590-45160-X

Text copyright © 1964 by Ann McGovern.
Illustrations copyright © 1992 by Scholastic Inc.
All rights reserved. Published by Scholastic Inc.

41 40 39 38 37   4 5 6/0

Printed in the U.S.A.   23

First Scholastic printing, May 1992

CONTENTS

When were colonial times?

Colonial times were a long time ago.

Colonial times began about seventy years after Columbus discovered America. They began when some settlers came from Spain to live in a colony in America. That was in the year 1565.

Colonial times ended when the thirteen English colonies became the United States. That was in the year 1776. This book does not tell about *all* the years that made up colonial times. It does not tell about *all* the thirteen colonies.

Look at the time line at the bottom of the page. The part that is in color shows the years this book is about.

Look at the map. The part that is in color is New England. This book is about life in the New England colonies.

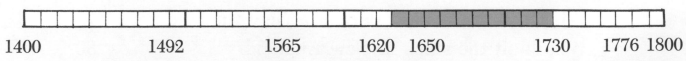

1400	1492	1565	1620	1650	1730	1776	1800

Columbus discovers America.

The first colony (St. Augustine, Florida) belongs to Spain.

The Mayflower lands at Plymouth.

The 13 colonies became the United States.

What was it like to live then? Did boys and girls in colonial times do the same things that you do today? Did they go to school? Did they have to worry about table manners? What did they do on Sundays? What games did they play? What happened if they got sick?

This book tells you. It also tells you about their work, their food, their houses, and their clothes.

This book will help you imagine what it was like to be a girl or a boy in colonial days.

The New England colonies later became the states of Connecticut, Rhode Island, Massachusetts, New Hampshire, Vermont, and Maine.

Vermont

Maine

New Hampshire

New York

Massachusetts

Rhode Island

Pennsylvania

Connecticut

New Jersey

What did colonial people look like?

When you look in the mirror, you see *you*.

If you lived in colonial days, you would look the same as you do now.

But you would wear your hair in a different way. And your clothes would be different, too. Even baby clothes were different then.

Clothes in colonial days had different names.

If a baby fell, he fell right on his *pudding!* A pudding was a soft pillow worn around the baby's middle to keep him from getting hurt.

When boys and girls were six years old, they stopped wearing baby clothes. From that time on they dressed just like their mothers and fathers.

Where did people buy their clothes?

Most people in colonial days did not buy their clothes any place. Most people made all their own clothes.

They planted flax to make linen thread. They raised sheep to get wool.

Everybody in the family helped to make the clothes. Grandmother's job was to card the wool.

The children gathered flowers and berries and roots to make the dyes to color the yarn.

People wore bright-colored clothes in colonial days — yellow, red, purple, blue. Girls wore bright-red cloaks and hoods. Boys wore gay-colored stockings and caps.

Girls and boys went to the woods and brought home armfuls of
— goldenrod and birchbark to make yellow dye
— pokeberry to make red
— iris to make purple
— logwood to make blue.

The dye was boiled in the biggest pot in the house. The children stirred the dye with a long stick, so it wouldn't get lumpy.

Girls and women worked at the spinning wheel. Girls learned to spin when they were six years old.

Younger sisters helped, too. They learned how to knit as soon as they could hold a pair of knitting needles. Girls of four could knit stockings and caps.

Boys and men did their share of work. Their job was to weave cloth on a loom. Then the women took the cloth and made clothes for the whole family. All the sewing was done by hand.

Was there a special time for making clothes?

The time for making clothes was all the time. People worked whenever they could.

When boys took the sheep to the fields, they took along a small loom. Then they could weave while they watched the sheep.

When women went visiting, they brought their spinning wheels along. They tied the spinning wheel to the back of their horse. Then they could spin while they visited. And no one could say they were wasting time!

How did they wear their hair?

Girls kept their hair covered all the time — even in the house. They wore hats and hoods or kerchiefs.

Boys had long hair. When wigs came into style, most men and even some boys in the big towns wore them. They wore wigs made of real hair, and wigs made from the tails of cows. They wore horsehair wigs and goathair wigs. They even wore wigs made of wire.

Some men put white powder on their wigs. On a windy day, the powder blew away like snow.

What did people eat?

Corn, corn, corn, and more corn!

Boiled corn and roasted corn. Corn ground into cornmeal and baked into corn cake and corn pudding.

The Indians taught the people how to plant corn and how to cook it. If there was nothing else to eat, the people could always count on corn.

But there *were* other things to eat. The people planted pumpkin and squash in the Indian way. The Indians showed them how to get maple sap from the maple trees. From the sap they made maple sugar and maple syrup, to sweeten their food.

There were no grocery stores in early colonial times — no place to buy food.

The people planted vegetables and fruit seeds that came all the way from Europe. They planted beans and trained them to climb up the cornstalks. They cooked the beans into a mush or porridge. And they ate bean porridge hot, bean porridge cold, and bean porridge in the pot nine days old.

The men and boys fished. They came home with lobsters, clams, and many other kinds of fish.

The men and the boys hunted. They came home with rabbits, squirrels, bear, and deer.

Some families kept a few pigs, so they could have bacon and pork and sausage.

During the cool days before winter, everybody worked extra hard. They had to get all their food ready for the cold months ahead.

Meat was smoked, salted, and pickled.

Apples and pumpkins and peaches were peeled and sliced and hung up to dry.

Later they would be cooked into stews or made into jams.

No one would be hungry.

No one would be thirsty, either.

There were not many cows in early colonial days, so there was not much milk. And people thought water would make them sick. What *did* they drink? They drank cider made from apples and pears and peaches.

And they drank beer. Children drank beer, too — even for breakfast!

Did children have to worry about table manners?

When you sit down to eat with your family, you are allowed to talk. If you lived in colonial days, you had to keep quiet.

You could not even sit down! You had to stand at the table all through the meal.

When supper was good, you could not say so.

When supper was bad, you could not say so either.

You could not say a word at the table. "Speak not" was a rule to remember.

There were many rules to remember.

"Sing not, hum not, wriggle not" was one rule.

Has your mother ever said to you, "Don't take such big bites. Don't make so much noise when you chew"?

There were the same rules in colonial days. All the rules were printed in a book of manners, and you had to learn them all.

The book of manners said, "Stuff not thy mouth to fill thy cheeks.

"Make not a noise with thy tongue, lips, or breath in thy eating or drinking."

It was good manners to eat with your fingers. There were spoons. But there were no forks until later colonial days. You used the same knife to cut your meat and to work with wood.

In many homes, one big pot was put on the table. Everyone put his spoon or his fingers into the pot to take out his food.

Your plate was a wooden board called a *trencher*. You shared your trencher with a sister or brother. You didn't have your own trencher. That would be too fancy!

Did children go to school?

Some did. Some didn't.

The first school that boys and girls went to in colonial days was called a Dame School. The teacher was a woman, and the children came to her house. In Dame School, children learned to read and write.

Did they have schoolbooks?

Older children used a book called the *New England Primer*.

Children in Dame School used a special kind of schoolbook called a *hornbook*. It was not a real book with pages to turn. It was a piece of wood with a printed page on each side of it.

The hornbook got its name from the thin sheet of horn that covered the page. You could see right through the horn.

As soon as the children learned to read and write everything that was on the hornbook, they were finished with Dame School.

Who learned more — girls or boys?

After Dame School, boys went on to another school to learn more. Girls stayed home.

Most people thought reading and writing were enough for girls to know. They thought it was more important for girls to know how to spin and cook and clean house.

But some people said, "Girls are as clever as boys. Why can't they learn, too?" So they taught their daughters at home.

Most boys had to go to school. The law said so. The law said every town with fifty families must build a school for boys. But some towns did not have enough money to build a school.

What were the schools like?

The law did not say schools had to be comfortable. And most of them weren't.

There were hard benches to sit on.

The school had only one room, which was freezing cold in the winter.

The only heat came from the fireplace. Every boy had to bring firewood for the fire. If he forgot, he had to sit far away from the fire. He had to sit in the coldest part of the room.

The family of every boy who went to school had to pay the schoolmaster. Often he was paid in corn or other food.

Sometimes the schoolmaster had more food than he could eat. That happened once to a schoolmaster in the town of Salem. The schoolmaster had too much corn. So he made one of the boys stand near an open window. When the boy saw someone walking by, he tried to trade the extra corn for something the schoolmaster could use.

There were no blackboards and no maps in colonial schools. There were no pencils, either. Boys wrote with a lump of lead. Or they wrote with a goose-quill pen dipped in homemade ink.

Paper was hard to get and cost a lot. Most boys wrote on birchbark. They could always get more in the woods. All they had to do was peel the bark off the birch trees.

Boys spent a lot of time learning to have nice handwriting. If they wrote their words clear and small, no one cared how the words were spelled. People spelled the same words in different ways. One school-master put a notice in the paper to say that he taught "writeing and spilling."

The *New England Primer* was the only schoolbook. It had many prayers. It had many questions and answers about God. And there were rhymes for each letter of the alphabet. For the letter D, the boys learned:

A Dog will bite
a thief at night.

As soon as the boys knew everything in the *New England Primer*, they could go to another school to learn more. Some boys were ready for college when they were only eleven years old. A few boys with rich fathers went to college in England.

But most boys stopped going to school. They went to work instead.

What happened if you didn't behave in school?

Almost every schoolmaster in colonial days kept a birch branch handy. And almost every schoolmaster used it to whip schoolboys who didn't behave.

They used other punishments, too.

If you didn't know your lessons, you were called a dunce. You had to sit on the dunce stool and wear a dunce cap. Sometimes you had to wear leather eyeglass frames.

If you whispered to a friend, you had to wear wooden *whispering sticks* in your mouth.

If you didn't pay attention to the schoolmaster, you

had to wear a card around your neck that said "Idle Boy."

If you were caught biting your nails, you had to wear a card that said "Bitefinger Baby."

Some punishments hurt your feelings and made you feel foolish. Some punishments just hurt!

A very cruel schoolmaster might tell a boy to bring him a small branch from a tree. The schoolmaster cut a slit in one end of the branch. The boy who didn't behave had to wear the branch on his nose for an hour or more.

If you went to school in colonial days and didn't behave — ouch!

BITEFINGER BABY

What books did children read?

The most important book was the Bible. Children were taught to read just so they could read the Bible.

There were many religious books.

There were serious books about manners.

And there were scary stories and poems about the terrible things that would happen to children who were not good.

But there were no storybooks for children. So children read storybooks that were written for grown-ups — *Aesop's Fables* and *Robinson Crusoe*.

What happened if you were sick?

If you were sick in colonial days, your mother would make you as comfortable as she could — just as your mother does now.

She would move your bed close to the fire to keep you warm. Then she would think about the kind of medicine to give you.

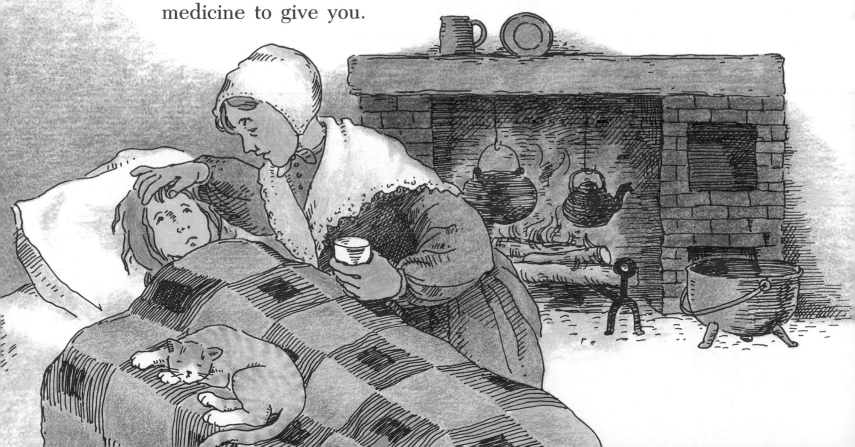

CHERVIL

HYSSOP

What kind of medicines did people use?

Plants called *herbs* were said to cure almost anything.

If you cut yourself, herbs made the cut heal faster.

If you bumped yourself, herbs made the swelling go down.

There were even herbs to help mend a broken arm or leg.

Every family grew their own herbs in their gardens and made their own medicines.

Herbs might be good for you, but they tasted bitter. Your mother would mix the herbs in honey to make them taste better.

Some people had strange ideas about medicines. A tea made of ground-up, roasted toads was supposed to be good for you.

Governor John Winthrop of Massachusetts Bay Colony wrote down what to do when someone had a high fever:

TEA

"Cut the sick man's nails and put the nails into a little bag of fine linen. Put a live eel into a tub of water. Tie the little bag of nails around the eel's neck. The eel will die, and the sick man will get better."

When a baby gets his first teeth, he often does not feel well. In colonial days, a mother would tie a string of berries around the baby's neck. This was supposed to make the baby feel better. But if the baby still cried, his mother tried another kind of necklace — a necklace made out of the teeth of a wolf!

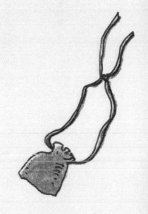

Anybody could sell medicines in colonial days. Sometimes the medicines that were sold were not medicines at all.

Some people sold plain water and called it medicine. They put water into a fancy bottle and gave it a fancy name.

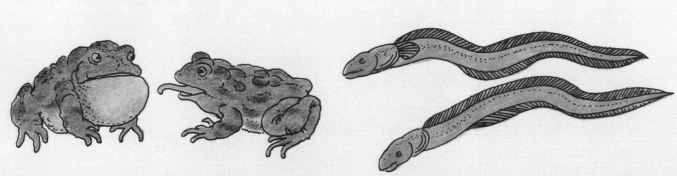

Were there doctors in colonial days?

There weren't many doctors. If you were very sick, your neighbor might be sent to get the nearest doctor. Your neighbor might have to ride all day before he found a doctor.

Many doctors thought a good way to cure a sick man was to bleed him. The doctor would cut open a vein in the sick man's arm and let some blood flow out.

If the sick man did not get better, people said it was the fault of witches. In colonial days many people believed in witches. They said that witches cast evil spells. It was the witches with their evil spells that made people sick, they said.

What happened if you went out at night?

If the town watchman saw you outside after dark, he might say, "What are you doing? Where are you going? You are supposed to be home."

And if you did not have a good reason, the town watchman would scold you and take you right home.

It was against the law to walk around at night. And it was the town watchman's job to see that everyone obeyed the law.

The town watchman never knew what he might have to do next.

Sometimes he had to take a lost cow home to its owner.

Sometimes he had to be a kind of alarm clock. If someone had to take a trip early in the morning, he would ask the town watchman to wake him up.

One town watchman walked the streets for three nights with a man who had such a bad toothache he could not sleep.

What did people do on Sunday?

Sunday was the Lord's Day.

It was a day to think about God. People thought about God at home. And they thought about God in their church, called a *meetinghouse*.

People went to the meetinghouse for two hours on Sunday morning. They went to the meetinghouse again for two hours Sunday afternoon.

Everybody had to go. Babies, too.

Babies who were too little to sit up straight on the wooden benches had a special place in the meeting-house. They were put in wooden cages, like playpens, where they could lie down.

Children tried not to wriggle around. They tried not to fall asleep during the long prayers, the Bible reading, the hymns, and the sermons.

What happened if you fell asleep in the meetinghouse?

If a baby fell asleep, no one cared. But if *you* fell asleep in the meetinghouse, you would get a rap on the head from the church watchman.

The watchman was called the *tithing-man*. It was his job to see that everyone paid attention. The tithing-man carried a long pole. On one end was a furry fox tail or a squirrel tail. On the other end was a wooden knob.

The tithing man used the wooden knob on the heads of children who fell asleep or talked or giggled.

He used the furry tail to tickle the noses of old men and women who fell asleep.

If anyone smiled or whispered in the meetinghouse, the tithing-man wrote down his name. The ones who smiled or whispered had to pay a fine.

Where did people eat on Sunday?

When the long morning service was over, it was time for lunch.

The people who lived far away from the meetinghouse did not go home for lunch. They went to the Sabbath House nearby.

Then back they went to the meetinghouse for the afternoon services.

At the end of the long day, the minister told the news of the week.

He had good news and he had bad news.

He told who was getting married and who had a new baby. He told who had broken the laws and had to be punished.

What laws did people have to obey?

There were laws that said no one should use bad words or get drunk.

It was against the law for a baker to bake bad bread. And it was against the law for a brewer to brew bad beer.

There were laws that said every man had to work on the town roads a few days each month. But many people did not obey this law. That is why the roads were so bad.

In one town there was even a law that said every man had to shoot three crows or twelve blackbirds between the middle of March and the last day of June. What was the reason for this law? The blackbirds and the crows ate the corn and the fruit.

There were special laws for poor people.

A poor man's clothes could not be as fancy as the clothes of a rich man.

The town of Boston had a law about dogs. The law said if a man was too poor to feed a dog, then he could not own one. A rich man could have only one dog.

There were laws for every day of the week. There were special laws for Sunday.

What were the special Sunday laws?

The most important Sunday law was the law that said everybody had to go to the meetinghouse on the Lord's Day.

On the Lord's Day, you could not laugh or play games.

No one could do any work. You could not even make your bed.

A man could not shave or cut his hair.

And it was against the law to kiss your mother or father on Sunday.

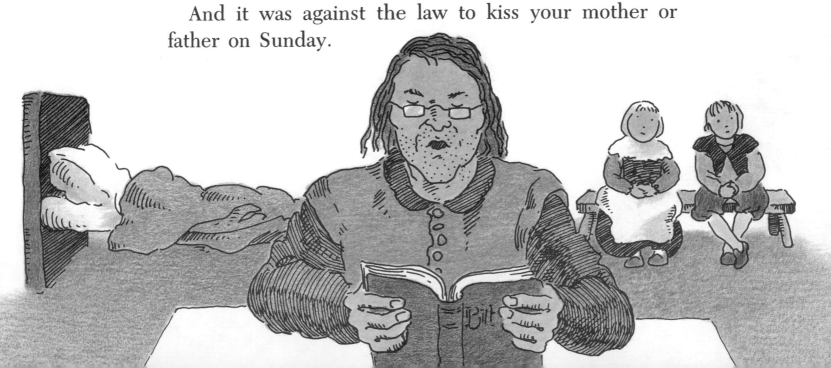

Who made all these laws?

The men of the town voted for the laws. They voted at a town meeting that was held at the meetinghouse. New laws were passed at the town meetings.

Could everyone vote in colonial days?

No. Women could never vote. And a man could vote only if he was a member of the church and if he owned land.

What happened to people who broke the laws?

People who broke the laws were punished. Punishments in colonial days were cruel. Hanging was a punishment for many crimes. If someone stole a silver spoon, he could be put to death.

Some people who broke the laws were whipped at the whipping post.

Some people were ducked in the water on a ducking stool. In colonial days it was against the law for a woman to talk back to her husband. If she did, she had to take the ducking-stool punishment.

Some people had to sit in the stocks. They had to wear cards around their necks that told what their crimes were.

To make the prisoners feel ashamed, the punishments took place out of doors — where everyone could see.

People who passed by made fun of the prisoners. They laughed at them. They threw rotten apples and mud at them.

It is said that the first man to sit in the Boston stocks was the carpenter who built them. What was his crime? He stole money to buy the lumber to make the stocks.

What did colonial houses look like?

Houses in early colonial days were not big or fancy. And they were not warm.

In wintertime, a colonial house was so cold that if you were writing a letter, the ink might freeze right on your pen!

To make the house warmer, the people burned giant logs in the fireplace.

Some logs were so big that it took two horses to drag them into the house.

How many rooms did a colonial house have?

Houses in early colonial days had one room. It was called the *keeping room.*

The family cooked and ate and worked in the keeping room. Here, too, the grown-ups and the babies slept. Older children slept in the attic.

Did big families live in big houses?

When more and more children were born, the family needed more and more space. So they built more rooms.

No matter how big the house was, the family still used the keeping room for cooking, eating, sleeping, and working.

There were many kinds of houses. One kind of house looked like the box in which salt was kept in colonial days. It is still called a *saltbox* house today.

What did the furniture look like?

Most people had plain furniture. They made it themselves. They didn't make much furniture because there was not much room to put it in.

In many houses there was only one chair. It belonged to the father. No one else was allowed to sit in it.

The rest of the family sat on wooden benches. Or they sat on the *settle*. The settle was a long wooden bench with high sides and a high back. It was not comfortable, but at least it was warm in winter. The high sides and the high back kept out the chilling winds that blew through the house.

What did people sleep on?

Mothers and fathers slept in a *jack-bed*. The jack-bed was short, to save space. Mothers and fathers did not sleep stretched out. The bed was not long enough.

The jack-bed was high, so that a smaller bed for the younger child could fit under it. The smaller bed was called a *trundle bed*. At night, the trundle bed was pulled out from under the jack-bed.

Babies slept in their cradles near the fireplace.

Older children slept in the attic on bags filled with scratchy straw. Or on softer mattresses filled with feathers or bits of wool.

Where did people hang their clothes?

People hung their clothes on pegs on the wall.

Where did people take baths?

There were no bathrooms in a colonial house. There was no running water, either.

People had to go outside the house for their water. They carried water home from the well in wooden buckets.

There was no way to make sure that the water was pure. So they did not often drink it. They did not often bathe in it, either.

When they *did* take a bath, they stood up in a big wooden tub of water in front of the fireplace.

Did people work hard in colonial days?

People *had* to work hard in colonial days. They had to, because almost everything they used they made themselves.

Think of the clothes the people wore.

There was spinning and weaving and knitting to be done. The spinning wheels and looms were home-made, too.

Think of the food they ate.

There were gardens to weed, rows and rows of corn to hoe, food to cook, bread to bake, butter to churn — no end to work!

Think of the dishes they used.

There were trenchers and bowls and spoons and mugs to make.

Think of the houses they lived in.

There were beds and tables and chairs and brooms and buckets and barrels to make. And when these things got broken, they had to be fixed.

Making soap and making candles took more than a day. Sometimes neighbors came to help and the job went faster.

When did boys and girls work?

Boys and girls were taught that work was good for them. In colonial days, people thought it was a sin to be lazy.

So every morning the children got up early and helped with the work. Boys worked before school, after school, and at night. Girls worked just as hard.

Did children have any time to play?

No matter how hard people worked, they always found some time to play. Colonial children did not have as much time to play as you do. But when they did play, they had just as much fun.

They played some of the games that you play today. They played tag and blindman's buff. They sang and played "Here We Go Round the Mulberry Bush" and "London Bridge Is Falling Down."

What games did boys like?

Most of all, boys liked to play ball. They played with
a leather ball filled with feathers.

Boys had tops to spin,
  drums to bang,
  popguns to pop.
They had hoops to roll,
  marbles to shoot,
  kites to fly.
They had trees to climb and icy ponds to skate on.
Their skates were made with wooden runners.

What did girls like to do?

Colonial girls played mostly with dolls. Their dolls were made of rags and cornhusks.

Some girls had wooden dolls. These dolls were not meant to be playthings. They were really fashion dolls. In big towns, like Boston, the dolls were put in shop windows. When a wooden doll got too old to be used in a shop window, it was given away to some lucky girl.

Girls sewed *samplers*. With tiny stitches, they made birds and trees and flowers and the letters of the alphabet. Girls made up mottoes for their samplers, like this one:

ABCDEFGHIJKLMNOPQRSTU
VWXYZ✱❀❀❀1234567891O
This is my Sampler

Here you see
What care my Mother
Took of me

Were there special days just for fun?

Sometimes, when crops were good and everybody had plenty to eat, the people had a holiday.

They set aside a special day to thank God for their good harvest. On that day, there was feasting and there was fun.

Sometimes, too, many families got together to help build a neighbor's house. When the house was finished, the people had a party to celebrate.

In many towns, a Training Day was held once a month. Men and boys ran races, held fighting matches, and took part in shooting contests. Prizes were given to the winners.

Were there special laws about fun?

In wintertime, coasting down snowy hills on sleds was against the law. Sledding was said to be a waste of time.

In the summer, in some towns, swimming was against the law. Swimming was said to be a waste of time, too.

Ministers gave long sermons against dancing. They said dancing was a sin. But their sermons did no good. People danced anyway. And in the large towns, dancing teachers gave lessons to children.

Did people travel much in colonial days?

No one in colonial days traveled just for fun. There was no easy way to travel.

There were no buses. No cars. No trains. No planes.

But there were wagons and horses and oxen and boats.

Boats were the best way to go.

Land travel was slow going. It was rough going, too.

Roads were narrow and bumpy and full of holes.

When it rained, the roads were muddy.

When it didn't rain, the roads were dusty.

And in the winter the roads were icy.

Roads in early colonial days were really Indian trails. They were so narrow that two people could not walk side by side.

How did people get across water?

On a horse.

On a bridge of stone or wood.

On a log. Most bridges were log bridges.
It was easy for an Indian to walk across a log bridge.
An Indian was used to it.

But a colonial man was not. And so he might find
himself *off* the bridge and *in* the water!

How did people travel when there was snow on the ground?

They traveled by *pod* and by *pung*. A *pod* was a sleigh pulled by one horse. A *pung* was a sleigh pulled by two horses.

People liked to travel in the snow. The snow filled in the holes in the road.

The wooden runners of the pods and the pungs went easily over the snow.

A trip might take a whole day — or longer. So travelers took their supper with them. And they took a potful of burning coals to cook it. They tied a big chunk of frozen bean porridge to the back of the sleigh. Whenever they got hungry, they chopped off a piece of porridge with their axes.

How did two men travel when they had only one horse?

Suppose there were two men and one horse.

One man was William and the other man was John. They wanted to get to the next town. But the horse was not strong enough to carry William and John at the same time.

How did they travel without riding the horse together?

The men started out at the same time. William rode the horse while John walked.

William rode for a few miles. Then he got off and walked. He left the horse tied to a tree. John came along. He got on the horse and rode past walking William. After a few miles, John got off the horse and tied it to a tree.

John and William took turns walking. They took turns riding and tying the horse.

This way of traveling was called ride-and-tie.

John did not get tired. Neither did William. Neither did the horse.

How did people get the news?

Most towns had a town crier. His job was to walk through the streets and call out the news of the day.

If the town crier had special news to tell, he rang a bell or banged on a drum. Then people ran to hear what he was saying.

Another way to hear the news was to go to the village inn. Travelers from other colonies told what was going on in their towns.

There were only a few newspapers in early colonial days. The papers printed news of the thirteen colonies. There was news about what ships were sailing and what cargo the ships carried. The papers also had poems, sermons, and advertisements.

How would you write a letter in colonial days?

Suppose your father was away from home, and you wanted to write to him. How would you begin your letter?

You would never write *Dear Dad*. That wouldn't be polite.

You would say *Dear Sir* or *Honour'd Sir*.

You would end the letter this way: *I am with greatest respect, Dear Father, Your dutiful Son* (or *Your dutiful Daughter*).

What would you use for a pen and ink and envelope?

You would write with a goose feather or a feather from a wild turkey. This was called a quill pen. Maple bark boiled in water made good ink.

To dry the ink, you would sprinkle sand over the page. There were no envelopes. So you would fold the letter. You would seal the folds with a blob of hot sealing wax.

Houses and streets had no numbers. So you might write the address like this:

To: Mr. William Bradgood
Near the White Horse Inn
In Cow Street
Boston

How would you send your letter?

Suppose you wanted to send your letter to someone in another colony. You would have to pay a man to deliver it. There was no regular mail service in early colonial days.

How long did it take to deliver a letter?

Sometimes it took the man a month to deliver a letter. In the wintertime the roads were bad. Then it took two months.

Sometimes the letter was never delivered. The man you hired might be killed by some Indians. Or his mailbag might fall into the river. That would be the end of your letter.

Sometimes it was easier and faster to send a letter to England than to send a letter to another colony. Sailing ships carried the mail to England in about four weeks.

When did the mail service get better?

The first regular mail service began in 1672, fifty-two years after the Pilgrims landed in Plymouth Rock. The mail was carried by men on horseback. The men were called *post riders.*

The post rider rode with the mail through forests, along narrow Indian trails, and across streams. He kept his gun loaded. There might be a hungry bear or a wolf nearby. Or an unfriendly Indian.

When the towns grew bigger, the roads became better. Then the mail was delivered by stage wagon. Travelers rode in the stage wagon, too.

When the wagon came to a big hill, the stage driver made all the passengers get out. They had to help push the wagon up the hill.

Who were the workers in a colonial town?

THE COBBLER

People in colonial days walked more than people do today. So they wore out their shoes faster.

Therc was always work for the town cobbler. He mended old shoes, and he made new shoes.

No one had to worry about left shoes and right shoes. The cobbler made all shoes exactly alike.

THE HATTER

The hatter made hats mostly from beaver skins.

THE BLACKSMITH

There was a blacksmith in every colonial town. The blacksmith made iron shoes for horses and for oxen. He made iron pots and nails and tools.

The blacksmith was a dentist, too. He had only one cure for toothaches. He pulled out the tooth that hurt!

THE PEWTERER

The pewterer made and mended pewter spoons, plates, and mugs.

THE TANNER

The tanner made leather from animal skins. In colonial days people wore leather breeches, leather aprons, leather caps, and leather boots.

They used leather buckets, rode on leather saddles, and drank from leather mugs.

The tanner was a busy man.

THE SILVERSMITH

The silversmith made silver spoons, plates, and cups.

There were no banks in colonial days. So instead of taking money to a bank, people brought their silver coins to the silversmith. The silversmith melted the coins and hammered them into beautiful silverware.

Paul Revere was a famous silversmith. Some of the silverware he made can be seen in museums.

THE CABINETMAKER

Most people in the country made their own furniture. But in the big towns, people built fancier houses. They wanted fancier furniture, too. The cabinetmaker made the furniture for them.

THE CLOCKMAKER

The clockmaker made the insides of the clocks. But he did not make the outside, called the *case*. People hung clocks without cases on the wall. These clocks were called *wag-on-the-wall* clocks.

If someone wanted a case for his clock, he went to the cabinetmaker. The cabinetmaker made cases for tall grandfather clocks and for smaller grandmother clocks.

THE MILLER

The miller ground corn and wheat into cornmeal and flour.

THE WHEELWRIGHT

The wheelwright made spinning wheels and wagons and carts.

THE COOPER

The cooper was a very important man in town. Everyone needed lots of barrels and buckets.

The cooper made barrels and buckets to hold salted fish and meat. He made barrels for rum and cider and beer and water.

THE BARBER

The colonial barber cut hair, of course.

He made wigs, too.

And if there were no doctors nearby, the barber was the doctor! His cure was to open a vein in a sick man's arm and let the blood flow into a pan. Most of the time this cure did no good. And often the sick man got worse instead of better.

THE TAILOR

Most people who lived in the country made their own clothes. They didn't need a tailor. But a tailor could always find work in big towns like Boston.

The tailor made clothes for the whole family. He sewed all the clothes by hand.

THE WHITESMITH

The whitesmith was sometimes called a tinsmith. He made tin candle-holders and tin foot warmers.

There wasn't much tin in early colonial days. So the whitesmith didn't make many new things of tin. He spent most of his time fixing broken tin.

What was the busiest part of a New England town?

The harbor was the busiest part of a New England town.

Ships sailed out of the harbor.

Ships sailed into the harbor.

Trading ships sailed out of the harbor. The ships carried fish, corn, candles, and other New England goods.

A few ships sailed across the ocean to England and to ports in Europe and Africa.

Some ships sailed along the Atlantic coast and traded with other colonies.

From the harbor fishermen set out to sea.

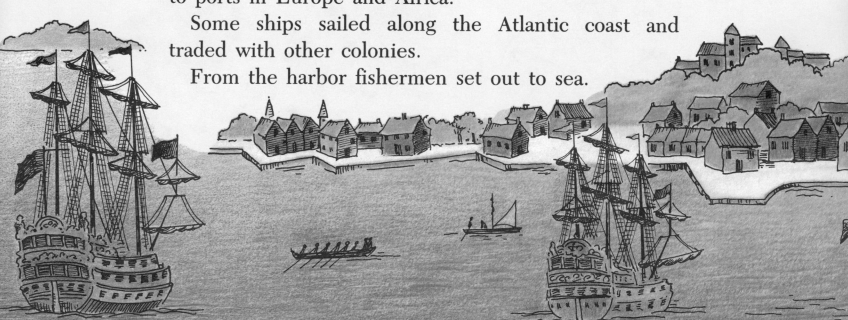

Ships sailed into the harbor.

Ships from England sailed into the harbor. They brought mail to the people of New England. They brought cargo, too. They might bring a fire engine for the town of Boston. Or a shiny coach for a rich man. Or a horse or two. Or the newest books printed in England.

Some ships brought people, too. They brought people who wanted to live in New England. These people were glad to come.

But some ships brought people who were not glad to come. These people came from Africa. They were sold as slaves, and they would never see their homes again.

Who built the ships in New England?

It took many kinds of workers to build the ships in New England.

Lumbermen cut down the tall pine trees to make the tall masts for the ships.

Carpenters built the wooden parts of the ships.

Ropemakers made ropes for the ships.

Sailmakers made the ships' sails.

Blacksmiths made nails and anchors and other hardware for the ships.

Coopers made barrels to hold food and drink for the long voyage.

Sailors and captains sailed the ships.

Ships and shipbuilding kept many, many men busy.